P9-DXE-325

THEY WERE THERE

A Guide to Firsthand Literature for Use in Teaching American History

By **RICHARD C. BROWN**

State University of New York College at Buffalo

SERVICE CENTER FOR TEACHERS OF HISTORY

A Publication of the American Historical Association
400 A Street, S.E. Washington, D.C. 20003

E
179
.B76
1962

© Copyright, THE AMERICAN HISTORICAL ASSOCIATION, 1962

All rights reserved. No part of this book may be reproduced in any form without permission in writing from the publisher, except by a reviewer who wishes to quote brief passages in connection with a review written for inclusion in a magazine or newspaper. The American Historical Association does not adopt official views on any field of history. The Service Center, following the tradition of the Association, does not necessarily agree or disagree with the views expressed in this book.

Library of Congress catalog card number: 62-13001

Composed and Printed at Waverly Press, Inc.
Baltimore, Maryland 21202

Printed in the United States of America

COMMITTEE ON TEACHING OF THE

AMERICAN HISTORICAL ASSOCIATION

JOSEPH R. STRAYER, *Chairman*
Princeton University

LOUIS B. WRIGHT (ex-officio)
Executive Secretary
American Historical Association

ROBERT R. COON
Alameda High School
Jefferson County R-1
Lakewood, Colorado

MISS MARGARETA FAISSLER
Roland Park Country School
Baltimore, Maryland

FRANK FREIDEL
Harvard University

STANLEY J. IDZERDA
Michigan State University

MRS. EUGENE MEYER
Washington, D. C.

JIM B. PEARSON
University of Texas

WILSON SMITH
University of California, Davis

LEFTEN S. STAVRIANOS
Northwestern University

OCT 7 - 1999

INTRODUCTION

Firsthand historical literature is written by people who saw or intimately experienced what they write about. It includes autobiographies, other personal narratives, diaries, travelers' accounts, letters, and some newspaper or magazine articles. A staggering amount of this kind of writing has been published and perhaps ten times as much remains unpublished. No one in a lifetime could possibly become acquainted with even the published firsthand literature of American history.

Yet any teacher and student of American history can, and should, become familiar with some of the better and more readily available examples of firsthand historical literature. Such literature has qualities that textbooks, monographs, and general histories rarely achieve. It can make the past vivid and real by distilling in words the flavor of the times when it was written. It can humanize the great historical figures and show as well that millions of ordinary persons also made history. It can lead the reader into fascinating byways of our nation's heritage, while deepening and broadening his knowledge of the better-known events.

This is not to say that firsthand literature is adequate as a total substitute for more formal history. It is usually too subjective and written too near the event to have the proper historical perspective. Still, used carefully as supplementary and enrichment material, it has a place in any classroom or home assignment in American history.

This pamphlet is a guide to firsthand historical literature that can be useful in teaching American history. Ways of using the material described herein are left to the energy and ingenuity of the teachers and students who read it. The guide is divided into two parts. Part One contains entries describing general collections of firsthand historical literature. Within each section of Part One, entries are arranged alphabetically according to the editors' names. However, the word "editor" is not repeated for each entry, except in one or two cases, it being understood that all the names listed are those of editors, rather than authors of firsthand literature. Part Two of the guide is devoted to firsthand literature written by one or two per-

1

119264

sons. In Part Two, the entries within sections are in alphabetical arrangement according to the author's name. Names of editors are included as part of the bibliographic information for each entry in Part Two.

For each entry, there is sufficient bibliographical information to enable librarians, teachers, students, or casual readers to buy or find the book in a library. Books out of print are indicated by the letters "o. p." If a book is published in a paperback edition, that fact is noted, although it is hard to keep up-to-date on paperback publications and prices. Each entry is accompanied by a short annotation which gives the nature of the work, the period covered, and other pertinent information.

Authenticity, availability, and interest rank equally in importance as criteria for inclusion in this pamphlet. Where there is serious doubt as to the authenticity of any entry, it is noted in the annotation. As to availability, most of the items included were published, or republished, within the last fifteen years. All the paperbacks and nearly all the clothbacked books are in print, according to Bowker's *Books in Print, 1961.* Many of both will be in a good secondary school library and many more can be found in a large public library system. The interest level aimed for is what Margareta Faissler called "pre-college readers" in the first pamphlet of the Service Center for Teachers of History series. Still, it is hoped that there is something here for all students and teachers of American history.

The criteria for inclusion reflect the compiler's judgment. He can only hope that the guide will provide one basic list, to which teachers and students can add as they see fit.

One special problem of published firsthand historical literature should be discussed. It has to do with both authenticity and interest. Very few writers of firsthand literature realized that twentieth-century eyes would someday be reading what they wrote. Naturally, these writers used the idiom, the spelling, the grammar, and the punctuation of their day. Moreover, they often included material which was of interest to them, but not particularly interesting to or instructive for today's readers. Most of the editors of works included in this guide were trying to make them available for and interesting to the twentieth-century reading public. Thus, in almost every case, language, spelling, and punctuation have been put in accord with modern usage. In many cases editors have left out or slightly changed parts of the original source, with no indication that they have done so. In this way, they have perhaps sacrificed some authenticity in favor of interest and readability. This problem is mentioned here to avoid discussing it in each annotation. Where abridgement or changes in language are noteworthy, the annotation indicates the nature of the change.

In conclusion it should certainly be said that this pamphlet makes no pretense of being an exhaustive guide to firsthand historical literature. For those who wish to develop augmented or additional lists of firsthand material, there are many other guides available. The *Harvard Guide to American History* (Harvard University Press, 1954) lists travelers' accounts in Section 48 and personal records of other kinds in Section 54. Richard G. Lillard's *American Life in Autobiography: A Descriptive Guide* (Stanford University Press, 1956) describes some four hundred works, selected to represent a sampling of the better autobiographies written by Americans in many different walks of life. *A Guide to the Study of the United States of America* (Government Printing Office, 1960) is rich in information about firsthand historical literature, but it takes some digging to gain its treasure.

RICHARD C. BROWN
*State University of New York
College at Buffalo*

PART ONE—GENERAL COLLECTIONS

A. Covering All, or Nearly All, of American History.
  1. Angle, Paul M. *The American Reader*. Rand McNally. 1958. 703 pp. $7.50.

     This broad collection contains some 250 selections, covering the years 1492 to 1958. The selections are from two to four pages long and deal with all facets of American history.
  2. Angle, Paul M. *The American Reader*. Fawcett. Five paperback volumes, 50¢ each.

     The five paperbacks contain the same selections as the hardcover edition. The volume titles are: I—*New Continent and a New Nation;* II—*The New Nation Grows;* III—*The Nation Divided;* IV—*Making of a World Power;* V—*Uneasy World*.
  3. Berger, Joseph, and Dorothy Berger. *Diary of America*. Simon and Schuster. 1957. 637 pp. $6.50.

     The Bergers have arranged excerpts from the diaries of 100 men and women in an attempt to tell our nation's history. The diarists range from colonial times to the 1940's. Most are significant historical figures, although ordinary persons who happened to keep diaries are also represented. Some excerpts may be a bit racy for less sophisticated students.
  4. Brown, Richard C. *The Human Side of American History*. Ginn. 1962. 320 pp. Paperback. $1.20.

     About 170 selections, covering the entire span of American history. The selections are short, from one to three pages, chronologically arranged, and stress human interest material.
  5. Commager, Henry S., and Nevins, Allan. *The Heritage of America*. Little, Brown. 1949. (Revised and enlarged edition) 1227 pp. $8.00.

     Published first in 1939, this collection has gone through two editions and a number of printings since then. Included are 269 selections, ranging in time from Leif Ericson to the atomic bombing of Japan and in length from two to eight pages. Social and cultural history are represented, although economic, political, and military history receive most emphasis.

6. Hart, Albert B. *American History Told By Contemporaries*. Macmillan. 1897–1929. Five volumes. $33.

This grandfather of twentieth-century collections of firsthand historical literature is still valuable. It concentrates more on political and economic selections. The volumes dealing with the early period of our history retain the spelling and language of the original documents. Each volume contains a discussion of sources and how to use them. Volume titles are: I—*Era of Colonization, 1492–1689;* II—*Building of the Republic, 1689–1783;* III—*National Expansion, 1783–1845;* IV—*Welding of the Nation, 1845–1900;* V—*Twentieth Century United States, 1900–1929.*

B. Collections Concerning the Exploration and Colonial Period.

1. Dorson, Richard M. *America Begins*. Pantheon. 1950. 438 pp. $4.50.

About 100 short selections from writers who are often included in source books of colonial literature. The collection gives intimate glimpses into English colonial life, mostly in the seventeenth century. While some selections tell of adventure, hardship, and torture, most are concerned with observations of God's wonder-working in daily lives of people.

2. Jameson, J. Franklin, general editor. *Original Narratives of American History*. Barnes and Noble. 1957. Nineteen volumes. $99.25 for complete set. $5.75 each.

These volumes were originally published in the early 1900's. They include travel and exploration accounts, chronicles, contemporary history and literature, court records, etc. Nearly always the complete manuscript is published with no deletions. Those translated from French, Spanish, or Dutch are in modern English while the English accounts appear pretty much in their original form. This may lead some readers to believe that Father Marquette, for example, could spell better and write better English than John Smith. Each volume is edited by an authority on its subject. Editors' names, volume titles, and period covered are:

Andrews, Charles M. *Narratives of the Insurrections, 1675–1690.* 487 pp.

Bolton, Herbert E. *Spanish Exploration in the Southwest, 1542–1706.* 487 pp.

Burr, George L. *Narratives of the Witchcraft Cases, 1648–1706.* 467 pp.

Burrage, Henry S. *Early English and French Voyages, Chiefly From Hakluyt, 1534–1608.* 451 pp.

Davis, William T. *William Bradford's "History of Plymouth Plantation," 1606–1646.* 437 pp.

Grant, William L. *Voyages of Samuel De Champlain, 1604–1618.* 377 pp.

Hall, Clayton C. *Narratives of Early Maryland, 1634–1684.* 460 pp.

Hodge, Frederick W., and Theodore H. Lewis. *Spanish Explorers in the Southern United States, 1528–1543.* 411 pp.

Hosmer, James K. *Winthrop's Journal "History of New England," 1630–1649.* (Two volumes)

James, Bartlett B., and J. Franklin Jameson. *Journal of Jasper Danckaerts, 1679–1680.* 313 pp.

Jameson, J. Franklin. *Narratives of New Nederland, 1609–1664.* 478 pp.

Edward Johnson's "Wonderworking Providence," 1628–1651. 285 pp.

Kellogg, Louise P. *Early Narratives of the Northwest, 1634–1699.* 382 pp.

Lincoln, Charles H. *Narratives of the Indian Wars, 1675–1699.* 382 pp.

Myers, Albert C. *Narratives of Early Pennsylvania, West New Jersey and Delaware, 1630–1707.* 476 pp.

Olson, Julius E., and Edward G. Bourne. *The Northmen, Columbus and Cabot, 985–1503.* 443 pp.

Salley, Alexander S. *Narratives of Early Carolina, 1650–1708.* 388 pp.

Tyler, Lyon G. *Narratives of Early Virginia, 1606–1625.* 478 pp.

C. Collections Concerning the American Revolution.
  1. Commager, Henry S., and Richard B. Morris. *The Spirit of 'Seventy-Six.* Bobbs-Merrill. 1958. Two volumes. $15.00.

There are over 1,000 short and varied selections in this collection. They cover all aspects of the period from 1765 through 1789. With something here for everyone, this is a collection to browse through.

2. Dorson, Richard M. *America Rebels*. Pantheon. 1953. 347 pp. $5.00.

This collection contains fourteen long narratives, some up to fifty pages in length. They include accounts of persons captured by the British or Indians, the Loyalist viewpoint, and glimpses of the fighting at Lexington, Saratoga, Vincennes, and Yorktown. Readers will be able to learn much about the war and the life of the times by reading any one of the selections, but once started they will have difficulty keeping from reading them all.

3. Scheer, George F., and Hugh F. Rankin. *Rebels and Redcoats*. World Publishing Company. 1957. 572 pp. $7.50.

Scheer and Rankin have drawn on a large body of firsthand literature from both sides in the Revolutionary struggle. However, they have presented only snippets of them, interspersed among their own narrative and transitional comments. The firsthand accounts are marked by stars, but it is sometimes difficult to tell which are firsthand accounts and which are the words of the editors. The whole book relates a connected, exciting story of the Revolution.

4. Scheer, George F., and Hugh F. Rankin. *Rebels and Redcoats*. New American Library. Paperback. 75¢

This contains the same material as the hardcover book.

D. Collections of Travelers' Accounts.

1. Commager, Henry S. *America In Perspective*. Random House. 1947. 389 pp. (o. p.)

Thirty-five extracts from the writings of foreign travelers in the United States between 1782 and 1945. Thirty-four of the accounts are by Europeans, mostly from the British Isles, and one was written by an Asiatic. The extracts are generally interpretative, rather than descriptive. They may not be lively enough for the average secondary school student, but good students can profit from reading in this collection.

2. Commager, Henry S. *America in Perspective*. New American Library. Paperback. 75¢.

An abridged edition of the hardcover book, designed to appeal to a wider audience.

3. Handlin, Oscar. *This Was America.* Harvard University. 1949. 602 pp. $4.50.

Forty extracts, including some translated into English for the first time. The collection features penetrating descriptions, with some critical comments, rather than interpretation. European travelers who visited America in the 18th, 19th, and 20th centuries are represented in this collection.

4. Nevins, Allan. *America Through British Eyes.* Oxford University. (New revised and enlarged edition.) 1948. 530 pp. (o. p.)

Most of this collection was first published in 1923 under the title *American Social History as Recorded by British Travellers.* The latest edition consists of long accounts, taken from the writings of thirty British travelers in the United States from 1794 to 1946. Nevins groups the accounts into periods. His introductory statements for each period give the general outlook as well as an individual description of each traveler.

5. Tryon, Warren S. *A Mirror For Americans.* University of Chicago. 1952. Three volumes. Boxed set, $14.50. $5.00 for each volume.

Tryon's collection covers the years 1790 to 1870. It consists of forty-three long extracts taken from accounts by Americans who traveled in and described their own country. Accounts of social and economic life are emphasized in the collection. Introductions to each account give the background of the traveler. Volume titles are: I—*Life in the East;* II—*The Cotton Kingdom;* III—*The Frontier Moves West.*

6. Tryon, Warren S. *My Native Land: Life in America, 1790–1870.* University of Chicago. Paperback. $1.95.

A shortened version of the three-volume collection listed above.

E. Collections Concerning the Civil War, North and South.

Commager, Henry S. *The Blue and the Gray.* Bobbs-Merrill. 1950. 1,151 pp. Two volume edition, $12.00. One volume edition, $8.95.

Comparable to *The Spirit of 'Seventy-Six* in the number and diversity of its selections. It covers the causes and every part of the war, life behind the lines, and even has a chapter on soldiers' songs and war-time poetry. The contents are almost equally divided between Confederate and Union locales.

2. Eisenschiml, Otto, and Ralph Newman. *The American Iliad.* Bobbs-Merrill. 1949. 720 pp. (o. p.).

Nearly two hundred eye witnesses and contemporaries are represented in this book. Their accounts are arranged to tell the military part of the war. The editors have provided sentences or paragraphs to provide transitions between the first-hand accounts. The total is somewhat disjointed, but interesting and dramatic.

3. Eisenschiml, Otto, and Ralph Newman. *Eyewitness: The Civil War As We Lived It.* Grosset & Dunlap. Paperback. $1.95.

Essentially the same material and the same format as *The American Iliad*, published as a paperback.

4. Harwell, Richard B. *The Confederate Reader.* Longmans, Green. 1957. 389 pp. $7.50.

Consisting of over fifty selections, arranged chronologically, this reader is designed to provide highlights of the Confederate States of America. There are a variety of selections: songs, some official documents, newspaper articles, and so on.

5. Harwell, Richard B. *The Union Reader.* Longmans, Green. 1958. 362 pp. $7.50.

On the same general pattern as *The Confederate Reader*, but dealing with the Union side of the war.

6. Jones, Katherine M. *Heroines of Dixie.* Bobbs-Merrill. 1955. 430 pp. $5.00.

A unique collection, giving the southern women's side of the war in their own words. One hundred and six selections, within nine chapters, arranged in chronological order from December, 1860 to May, 1865. Some of the selections are by women who served as nurses or spies. Most, however, are by women who lived, worked, and waited behind the lines, and these portray the heartbreak of the home front.

7. Nichols, Roy F. *Battles and Leaders of the Civil War.* Yoseloff.

1957. Four volumes. Boxed set, $30. Popular Edition, $4.95 for each volume.

For those who like their military history in the words of leading participants, written twenty years after the events they describe. This edition is condensed from the original edition issued in several volumes during the 1880's. The titles of the four volumes are: I—*From Sumter to Shiloh;* II—*North to Antietam;* III—*Retreat from Gettysburg;* IV—*The Way to Appomattox.*

F. Collections Concerning the Trans-Mississippi West.

    1. Blegen, Theodore C., and Philip D. Jordan. *With Various Voices; Recordings of North Star Life.* Itasca Press. 1949. 372 pp. (o. p.).

        Fifty-four selections, arranged within eleven sections to tell the story of Minnesota history from early exploration through the nineteenth century.

    2. Emrich, Duncan. *Comstock Bonanza.* Vanguard. 1950. 363 pp. (o. p.).

        A collection of more than thirty articles and stories from the works of J. Ross Browne, Mark Twain, Bret Harte, Dan de Quille and others. Taken from rare periodicals and out-of-print books, the selections picture life on the early mining frontier of Nevada.

    3. Graham, W. A. *The Custer Myth: A Source Book of Custeriana.* Stackpole. 1953. 413 pp. $10.00.

        This includes about all the eye-witness evidence there is on the Custer massacre at the Little Big Horn, even accounts by Indians who were there. The compiler presents evidence on both sides, pro- and anti-Custer. The volume concludes with mournful descriptions of the burial and reburial of the massacred cavalrymen.

    4. Hamilton, Charles. *Cry of the Thunderbird; the American Indians' Own Story.* Macmillan. 1950. 283 pp. $4.50.

        Indian versions of their way of life and their views of the whites. Most of the selections are short, consisting mainly of nineteenth-century accounts by Indians living west of the Mississippi.

5. Lewis, Oscar. *The Autobiography of the West*. Holt. 1958. 306 pp. (o. p.).

Selections are short, not footnoted, and are arranged in chapters. Lewis' comments are interspersed in an attempt to tell a connected story from the days of the early Spanish explorers to the completion of the trans-continental railroads.

6. Westermeier, Clifford P. *Trailing the Cowboy: His Life and Lore as Told by Frontier Journalists*. Caxton Printers. 1955. 414 pp. $5.00.

A collection of pieces from newspapers, magazines, and books contemporary with the old-time cowboys. Selections are in both prose and verse. Every aspect of cowboy life and every point of view is represented.

G. Other Collections.

1. Blegen, Theodore C. *Land of Their Choice: The Immigrants Write Home*. University of Minnesota. 1955. 463 pp. $5.75.

A collection of Norwegian immigrants' letters written from many parts of the United States between 1825 and 1869 to friends and relatives in Norway. In the letters, the immigrants reveal much of themselves, but also much about transportation as well as city and farm life and work in the United States during the period. Although other volumes of immigrant letters have been compiled and published, this is perhaps the most interesting and intelligently edited.

2. Botkin, B. A. *Lay My Burden Down; A Folk History of Slavery*. University of Chicago. 1961. Paperback. $1.65.

In anecdote and folk tale, former Negro slaves tell what slavery and emancipation meant to them. These personal recollections of slavery days vary widely, according to the informants' individual experiences.

3. Danzig, Allison, and Peter Brandwein. *The Greatest Sports Stories From the New York Times*. A. S. Barnes. 1951. 658 pp. (o. p.).

Nearly two hundred selected eye-witness accounts of the most celebrated events in the field of sports between 1851 and 1951. Taken from the files of the *New York Times*, the selections deal with many different kinds of sporting events. In so doing, they relate a surprising amount of American social history.

4. Meyer, Robert F. *The Stars and Stripes Story of World War II.* McKay. 1961. 504 pp. $5.95.

   The story of World War II as told by firsthand accounts from the U. S. servicemen's own paper. *The Stars and Stripes* began publication in April, 1942 and this collection consists of articles from then until September, 1945. Arranged in chronological order, the selections are woven into a connected story through bridging material provided by the editor.

5. Mulder, William, and A. Russell Mortensen. *Among the Mormons: Historic Accounts by Contemporary Observers.* Knopf. 1958. 482 pp. $6.75.

   About one hundred selections enable us to see the Mormons as contemporaries have seen them from their beginnings to the present day. The selections average four pages and almost all are by non-Mormons.

6. Shannon, David A. *The Great Depression.* Prentice-Hall. 171 pp. Paperback. $1.95.

   The story of the great depression, 1929–1941, told in human terms. Fifty-six accounts taken from newspapers, books, magazines, and governmental records. This collection recreates the meaning of depression for young people who have known only prosperity.

7. Still, Bayrd. *Mirror for Gotham.* New York University. 1956. 417 pp. $7.50.

   A panorama of New York from 1524 to the present, pictured by the words of hundreds of observers, distinguished and otherwise. Selections are short and arranged chronologically.

8. Stone, Irving. *We Speak For Ourselves.* Doubleday. 1950. 462 pp. (o. p.).

   Selections from 64 autobiographies chosen to represent the essence of the lives of the subjects. One or two sentence introductions tell only who the writer was. Autobiographical excerpts date from colonial times to the mid-twentieth century.

9. Syrett, Harold C., and Jean G. Cooke. *Interview in Wee-hawken: The Burr-Hamilton Duel as Told in the Original Documents.* (Introduction and conclusion by Willard M. Wallace.) Wesleyan University. 1960. 178 pp. $3.75.

   Accounts by the Burr and Hamilton seconds and other documents are skillfully edited to provide a moving story with continuity and suspense. This collection effectively recreates the atmosphere of the time and permits the reader to judge for himself the issues raised by the tragic duel.

10. *Selected Source Materials for College Research Papers.* Heath. 1956–1960. Paperback. $1.40 each.

   Each volume of this series contains from five to fifteen eye-witness accounts in about 120 pages. The pagination of the original sources and other bibliographic information is given for each selection. An introduction in each volume tells how to write a research paper. Although the materials are labeled for "college research papers," they are interesting and informative in themselves and are not too difficult for advanced high school students.

   Editors, titles, and dates of publication for those volumes suitable in teaching American history are:

   a. Anderson, Sylvia F., and Jacob Korg. *Westward to Oregon.* 1958.
   b. Bartel, Roland, and Edwin R. Bingham. *America Through Foreign Eyes, 1827–1842.* 1956.
   c. Bingham, Edwin R. *California Gold.* 1959.
   d. ———. *The Fur Trade in the West, 1815–1846.* 1960.
   e. Kogan, Bernard R. *The Chicago Haymarket Riot.* 1959.
   f. McCormick, Edgar L., and Edward G. McGehee. *Life on a Whaler.* 1960.
   g. McDonnell, Robert F., and William E. Morris. *Modern America Through Foreign Eyes.* 1959.

PART TWO—INDIVIDUAL ACCOUNTS

A. Accounts Originally Written During the Eighteenth Century.
1. Adams, Abigail. *New Letters.* Edited by Stewart Mitchell. Houghton Mifflin. 1947. 281 pp. $6.00.

   A noteworthy letter writer for her own or any other age, Mrs. Adams wrote these letters to her sister between 1788–1801. They reveal social, political, and domestic scenes during the Federalist Period, because Mrs. Adams was always at her husband's side while he served as Vice-President and President.
2. Adams, John and Abigail. *Familiar Letters of John Adams and His Wife, Abigail Adams, During the Revolution.* Edited by Charles Francis Adams. Hurd & Houghton. 1876. 424 pp. (o.p.).

   Though long out of print, these letters give a delightful picture of the Revolution as seen by a highly involved and highly intelligent husband and wife. A wealth of material on economic and personal matters is included.
3. Allen, Ethan. *Narrative of Colonel Ethan Allen.* Introduction by Brooke Hindle. Citadel. 1961. Paperback. $1.25.

   Revolutionary War memoirs of the hero of Fort Ticonderoga and leader of the Green Mountain Boys, first printed in 1779. Original language has been changed somewhat but enough remains to give the flavor of the times and of the unusual man who wrote the narrative.
4. Franklin, Benjamin. *The Autobiography and Other Writings.* Introduction by L. Jesse Lemisch. New American Library. Paperback. 50¢.

   There are many editions of Franklin's famous autobiography. This one reproduces the definitive Farrand text and also contains over 150 pages of other writings by Franklin.
5. Hamilton, Dr. Alexander. *Gentleman's Progress: The Itinerarium of Dr. Alexander Hamilton, 1744.* Edited with an Introduction by Carl Bridenbaugh. University of North Carolina. 1948. 267 pp. $4.00.

   This is a lively, witty, and highly instructive travel

account. Dr. Hamilton, not to be confused with the Federalist Secretary of the Treasury, traveled through the colonies to the north of his home in Maryland. His story of the journey in 1744 has been called the best travel account written in colonial America.

6. Jefferson, Thomas, *Autobiography of Thomas Jefferson.* Introduction by Dumas Malone. Putnam. 1959. 119 pp. Cloth, $2.50. Paperback, 95¢.

Begun when Jefferson was 77, this book gives his recollection of certain facts and events connected with his career. By no means a complete autobiography, it nevertheless reveals insight into the life of the great man.

7. Rogers, Robert. *Journals of Major Robert Rogers.* Citadel. 1961. Paperback. $1.50.

Written by the versatile eighteenth-century explorer, Indian fighter, and dramatist. These journals furnished Kenneth Roberts with part of his source material for his historical novel *Northwest Passage.*

8. Washington, George. *Journal of Major George Washington.* Edited by James R. Short and Thaddeus W. Tate, Jr. Colonial Williamsburg. 1959. $2.00.

A facsimile edition of the journal kept by the young Virginian as he prepared to warn the French away from the Ohio River country, thus helping to start the French and Indian War.

B. Accounts Originally Written Between 1800 and 1860.

1. Barnum, Phineas T. *Barnum's Own Story.* Dover. 1961. Paperback. $1.65.

Edited from *Struggles and Triumphs; The Life of P. T. Barnum, Written By Himself,* first published in 1855, and numerous later editions of Barnum's autobiography. This tells, in the language you would expect, the life of the greatest showman of the nineteenth century.

2. Crockett, David. *Adventures of Davy Crockett, Told Mostly by Himself.* Scribner. 1955. 246 pp. $3.75.

An abridgement of three narratives, supposedly written by the "original humorist and irrepressible backwoodsman," put together to appeal to young people.

3. Dana, Richard Henry. *Two Years Before the Mast: A Personal Narrative.* Modern Library Edition. $1.95. Doubleday Dolphin. Paperback. 95¢.

The classic account of ships and sailing during the early nineteenth century.

4. Douglass, Frederick. *Narrative of the Life of Frederick Douglass, An American Slave.* Edited by Benjamin Quarles. Belknap. 1960. 163 pp. $3.50.

Autobiography of the escaped slave who became an abolitionist orator and author, first published in 1845.

5. Forten, Charlotte. *Journal of Charlotte L. Forten.* Edited by Ray Allen Billington. Dryden. 1953. 162 pp. (o. p.).

An intensely written journal of a Philadelphia-born free Negro girl who attended normal school in Salem, Massachusetts during the 1850's. Her writing shows her interest in abolitionism and learning. Later she became a teacher of newly-freed slaves and her experiences in this role are interesting and instructive.

6. Houston, Sam. *The Autobiography of Sam Houston.* Edited by Donald Day and H. H. Ullom. University of Oklahoma. 1954. 298 pp. $5.00.

Consisting of extracts from Houston's speeches and writing, this "autobiography" gives the most colorful, dramatic, and interesting facets of Houston's life. The selections are woven together by editorial comment.

7. Jefferson, Isaac. *Memoirs of a Monticello Slave: As Dictated to Charles Campbell in the 1840's by Isaac, One of Thomas Jefferson's Slaves.* Edited by Rayford W. Logan. University of Virginia. 1951. 45 pp. $3.00.

Portraying Jefferson and his family from a unique viewpoint, these recollections also reveal something of Virginia slave life in the late eighteenth and early nineteenth century.

8. Lewis, Meriwether, and William Clark. *The Journals of Lewis and Clark.* Edited by Bernard De Voto. Houghton Mifflin. 1953. 504 pp. $6.50.

An abridged, readable version of the original record kept by the explorers on their historic mission. The essential narrative remains, but the editor omits the long descriptive passages which are often most interesting. De Voto has, however, retained much of the original spelling and readers will admit that some of the spelling is quite original.

9. Ma-Ka-Tai-Me-She-Kia-Kiak. *Black Hawk: An Autobiography*. Edited by Donald Jackson. University of Illinois. 1955. 180 pp. $3.75.

Black Hawk dictated his life's story to a government interpreter, Antoine Le Claire, and the story was put into written form by a young Illinois newspaperman, J. B. Patterson. Because of this process, historians have doubted the complete authenticity of the "autobiography," which first appeared in 1833. The editor of this handsomely illustrated and printed edition has carefully explained in footnotes the parts on which doubts have been expressed. High school students will enjoy Black Hawk's story of his youth, his version of the Black Hawk War, and his reactions to the sights he saw on a trip through the eastern states after the war ended.

10. Parkman, Francis. *The Oregon Trail*. Modern Library Edition. $1.95. New American Library. Paperback. 50¢.

Writing in his masterful style, Parkman tells of his experiences with immigrant trains and Indians on the northern plains during the late 1840's.

C. Individual Accounts Dealing With the Civil War Period.

1. Alcott, Louisa May. *Hospital Sketches*. Hill and Wang. Paperback. $1.25.

Based upon her experiences as a volunteer nurse in the early years of the war, these are some of the first published writings of the author of *Little Women* and *Little Men*. Originally published in *Commonwealth* magazine, they first appeared in book form in 1863. Sometimes humorous, sometimes tragic, they are always interesting, and show the state of medicine and hospitalization at the war's beginning.

2. Brobst, John F. *Well, Mary: Civil War Letters of a Wisconsin Volunteer*. Edited by Margaret Brobst Roth. University of Wisconsin. 1960. 165 pp. $4.00.

Letters of Private John F. Brobst, Twenty-fifth Wisconsin

Infantry, written 1862–1865. Brobst saw service at Vicksburg and with Sherman during the famous march across Georgia and northward through South Carolina. Informative and colorful, the letters give the common Union soldier's viewpoint of the war.

3. Chesnut, Mary Boykin. *A Diary From Dixie*. Edited by Ben Ames Williams. Houghton Mifflin 1949. 572 pp. Cloth cover, $7.50. Paperback, $2.50.

Mary Chesnut was a South Carolinian belle, wife of a United States senator who became a brigadier general in the Confederate Army. She was well acquainted with the Confederate leaders and wrote perhaps the most interesting, informative, and candid of all the memoirs and diaries of the Confederacy. Hardly anything escaped her attention, from affairs of state to love affairs of her friends.

4. Cumming, Kate. *Kate: The Journal of a Confederate Nurse*. Edited by Richard B. Harwell. Louisiana State University. 1959. 321 pp. $6.00.

Originally published in 1866, this remains as one of the best sources on the medical and social history of the Confederacy.

5. Douglas, Henry Kyd. *I Rode With Stonewall*. Fawcett. Paperback. 75¢.

These lively war experiences of Jackson's youngest staff officer were written during and after the Civil War. Douglas' account shows the genius of Jackson and the high morale of the Confederate foot soldier throughout most of the war.

6. Eggleston, George Cary. *A Rebel's Recollections*. With an introduction by David Donald. Indiana University. 1959. 192 pp. $3.75.

Brother of the man who wrote *The Hoosier Schoolmaster*, this Eggleston moved to Virginia in the 1850's and remained to fight for his adopted state. He wrote these urbane, intelligent recollections more than ten years after the end of the war. They tell a great deal about the economic collapse of the Confederacy.

7. Fremantle, Lt. Col. James Arthur Lyon. *The Fremantle Diary*.

Edited by Walter Lord. Little, Brown. 1954. 304 pp. $4.00.
Paperback, Capricorn. $1.35.

In spite of the author's military title (he was an officer of
the English Coldstream Guards) this deals with other than
military aspects of Confederate life. He traveled for three
months in 1863 through all the Confederate states except
Arkansas and Florida. *The Fremantle Diary* has been called
"by far the most interesting and well-written travel account
of life in the Confederacy." First published in London in
1863, it was very popular in the Confederacy when it
appeared there the following year.

8. Grant, Ulysses S. *Personal Memoirs.* Edited by E. B. Long.
World Publishing Company. 1952. 608 pp. (o. p.).

Clear and unpretentious, these memoirs of Grant's
Mexican and Civil War experience are for students interested
in military history. First published in 1885–86, they were
written by Grant to provide an estate for his family. He
completed them, after eleven months of work, just a week
before he died of cancer of the throat.

9. Green, John. *Johnny Green of the Orphan Brigade: The Journal
of a Confederate Soldier.* Edited by Albert D. Kirwan. University of Kentucky. 1956. 214 pp. $3.50.

This is one of the best of the common soldier accounts of
of the war. Green was a plain little fellow with a quaint
sense of humor and enduring courage. These qualities show
through in his journal.

10. Halstead, Murat. *Three Against Lincoln: Murat Halstead
Reports the Caucuses of 1860.* Edited with an introduction by
William B. Hesseltine. Louisiana State University, 1960.
321 pp. $6.00.

Murat Halstead was a correspondent for the Cincinnati
Commercial who wrote reports on the Democratic conventions
of 1860 in Charleston and Baltimore, as well as the Republican convention in Chicago that nominanted Lincoln. His
reports on the Democratic conventions are objective, but he
favored Seward over Lincoln for the Republican nomination. For this reason, his account of the Republican con-

vention will be an eye-opener for students who think of Lincoln as an honest rail splitter or as a statue enshrined in the Lincoln Memorial.

11. Jones, John B. *A Rebel War Clerk's Diary.* Edited by Earl Schenck Miers. A. S. Barnes. Paperback. $2.45.

Jones was a clerk for the Confederate government, working in a Richmond office throughout the war. This is an abridgement of his diary, originally published in two volumes in 1866. Its revelations of Confederate bungling, written from the unique viewpoint of Jones's humble position, have been called "a worm's eye view of the war."

12. Le Conte, Emma. *When the World Ended: The Diary of Emma Le Conte.* Edited by Earl Schenck Miers. Oxford University. 1957. 124 pp. $4.00.

Emma Le Conte was seventeen and living in Columbia, South Carolina when she wrote this remarkable diary. It records tragic events in her home town during the winter and spring of 1865 while General Sherman was coming. In the diary we see the war through the eyes of a young girl.

13. McElroy, John. *Andersonville: A Story of Rebel Military Prisons.* Fawcett. Paperback. 75¢.

An abridgement of the author's recollections, first published in 1879. McElroy, who had been a prisoner at Andersonville, tells of great human suffering and equally great courage.

14. Russell, William Howard. *My Diary North and South.* Edited with an introduction by Fletcher Pratt. Harper. 1954. 268 pp. $4.50.

War correspondent for the London *Times*, Russell interviewed Union and Confederate leaders during the early months of the war. His truthful report of the Union rout at Bull Run aroused indignation in the North and he was forced to return to England early in 1862. There his diary was published in 1863. This is a drastic reduction of the original, but it does contain Russell's graphic description of Bull Run.

15. Semmes, Raphael. *The Confederate Raider, Alabama.* Edited by Philip Van Doren Stern. Fawcett. Paperback. 75¢.

This book consists of selections from a longer work by

Semmes, who was commander of the *Alabama*. They help make the famous "Alabama Claims Case" real by telling the dramatic story of the Confederate raider whose sorties inflicted such heavy losses upon Union shipping during the Civil War.

16. Stone, Kate. *Brokenburn: The Journal of Kate Stone, 1861–1868.* Edited by John Q. Anderson. Louisiana State University. 1955. 400 pp. $4.95.

The warm, chatty, exciting observations of an intelligent young woman who was twenty when she started her journal in May, 1861. The author lived in Louisiana and then fled to Texas when Union soldiers overran the Stone plantation. The journal is fullest for the war years and contains little of interest for the three years following.

17. Trowbridge, John T. *The Desolate South, 1865–1866.* Duell, Sloan and Pearce. 1956. 320 pp. $6.00.

Trowbridge was one of the many Yankee reporters who flocked into the South when the war ended. He made a four-months' tour of the most famous battlefields, reporting in colorful, almost photographic, fashion how they looked as the work of reconstruction began. This contains about half the original Trowbridge material, first printed in 1866.

D. Individual Accounts Concerned Chiefly With Some Part of the Period 1865–1920.

1. Addams, Jane. *Twenty Years at Hull House.* New American Library. Paperback. 75¢.

A classic, first published in 1910. It combines autobiography, an account of the establishment and growth of the famous settlement house on Halsted Street in Chicago, and Miss Addams' concern with various reform movements, particularly feminism and pacifism.

2. Antin, Mary. *The Promised Land.* Houghton Mifflin. 1929. 373 pp. $5.00.

An immigrant's autobiographical account, dealing mainly with the situation of Jews in the United States as contrasted with that of Jews in Europe.

3. Betzinez, Jason. (With W. S. Nye) *I Fought With Geronimo.* Stackpole. 1959. 214 pp. $4.95.

This interesting book contains recollections of Apache

reservation life, Indian warfare in the Southwest, and the educational program at Carlisle Indian School, where the author finally adapted to the white man's ways.

4. Carnegie, Andrew. *The Autobiography of Andrew Carnegie.* Houghton Mifflin. 469 pp. $5.00.

   Latest edition of the life story of the canny little Scotsman who became America's steel king. The latter part of the book gets rather philosophical; but the earlier chapters, dealing with Carnegie's younger days, remarkably reveal his personality and the America in which he lived.

5. Garland, Hamlin. *A Son of the Middle Border.* Macmillan. 1923. 402 pp. $4.95.

   Garland's brilliantly written recollections evoke a realistic picture of late nineteenth-century farm life in Wisconsin, Iowa, and the Dakota Territory and its effect on his own family.

6. Gompers, Samuel. *Seventy Years of Life and Labor.* Edited by Philip Taft and John A. Sessions. Dutton. 1957. 621 pp. $5.00.

   A cut-down version of Gompers' autobiography which was originally published in two volumes. This work eliminates much of the dated material but still preserves the parts that tell of Gompers' life and of the early history of the American Federation of Labor.

7. Hoover, Herbert. *The Memoirs of Herbert Hoover.* Macmillan. 1953. Three volumes. $6.00 each.

   The first volume, *Years of Adventure, 1874–1920*, is likely to be by far the most interesting to younger readers. It tells of Hoover's boyhood in Iowa and Oregon, his education at Stanford, his highly successful career as a mining engineer and engineering consultant, and the impressive story of his humanitarian work, relieving hunger and suffering in Europe during and immediately after World War I. The second volume is titled *Cabinet and the Presidency, 1920–1933;* the third, *Great Depression, 1929–1941.* They contain Hoover's thoughts at the time he was experiencing the events of the period covered. Apparently, he saw no reason to change them in any way when his memoirs were published.

8. Macrae, David. *The Americans At Home*. Dutton. 1952. 469 pp. (o. p.).

First published in England in 1871, this is an excellent travel account for fairly sophisticated readers. It was written by a Scottish clergyman who traveled in Canada, the East, the South, and on the Mississippi River during the late 1860's. Written well and humorously, Macrae's account is full of jokes, anecdotes, and acute observations.

9. Nelson, Klondy. (With Corey Ford). *Daughter of the Gold Rush*. Random House. 1958. 387 pp. $3.50.

Klondy Nelson, whose father was a roving prospector, gives a child's picture of life during the Alaskan gold rushes as she remembered it more than fifty years after.

10. Pupin, Michael. *From Immigrant to Inventor*. Scribner. 1949. 396 pp. Cloth cover, $3.95. Paperback, $1.45.

A peasant's son from a south-central European village, the author came to America at the age of sixteen. He eventually became professor of electromechanics at Columbia University and the inventor of many improvements in telegraphy, telephony, and the X-ray. This success story was a best-seller in the 1920's and received a Pulitzer prize.

11. Rogers, Will. *The Autobiography of Will Rogers*. Selected and edited by Donald Day. Houghton Mifflin. 1949. 462 pp. $5.00.

This is a "manufactured" autobiography, put together by the editor from Will's speeches, daily newspaper columns, stage performances and books. Inserted editorial comment provides a connected life story of the cowboy humorist and his role as a beloved commentator on public affairs.

12. Roosevelt, Theodore. *The Autobiography of Theodore Roosevelt*. Centennial Edition. Edited with an introduction by Wayne Andrews. Scribner. 1958. 561 pp. $4.95.

Good readers will enjoy Roosevelt's tales of his life in the West and all readers can get a taste of the vigorous Roosevelt personality from this autobiography.

13. Roosevelt, Theodore. *The Rough Riders*. New American Library. Paperback. 50¢.

Roosevelt's Spanish-American War experiences told in his own red-blooded prose.

14. Sinclair, Upton. *The Jungle*. New American Library. 50¢.

This famous exposé of conditions in the Chicago stockyards at the turn of the century, based on Sinclair's personal observations, is still affecting today.

15. Steffens, Lincoln. *The Autobiography of Lincoln Steffens*. Harcourt, Brace. 1936. 873 pp. $7.50. Abridged edition, $2.50. Abridged text edition, $1.75.

The full edition relates the vivid and candid life story of the eminent journalist who was in the front ranks of the Muckrakers and a brilliant student of ethics and politics. It is one of the finest of all modern autobiographies. The abridged editions eliminate much of the controversial material from Steffens' later life, particularly his opinions on world affairs, which have become somewhat dated.

16. Steffens, Lincoln. *The Shame of the Cities*. Hill and Wang. Paperback. $1.25.

This contains the complete text of the famous muckraking accounts of corrupt government in America's leading cities. Steffens wrote them after making personal visits and inquiries during the early years of the twentieth century.

17. Twain, Mark. *Mark Twain's Picture of His America*. Selected and edited by Neal F. Doubleday. Heath. Paperback. $1.40.

Thirteen selections from Twain's writing depicting the great days of Mississippi steamboating, Twain's brief experience in a Confederate militia unit, flush times in the Nevada silver mines, and containing observations on the Gilded Age. One of the *Selected Source Materials for College Research Papers* series. (See Part One, G, 10.)

18. Twain, Mark. *Roughing It*. Rinehart. Paperback. 95¢.

Saga of boom towns, silver rushes, land-grabbing and boisterous life on the western frontier in the early 1860's as the author experienced it. First published in book form in 1872.

19. Washington, Booker T. *Up From Slavery*. Doubleday. 1951. 244 pp. $3.50.

Originally published in 1900, this deals mainly with the

early life of the famed president of Tuskegee Institute in Alabama. By 1900, Washington had become recognized as a great leader of the American Negro. He advocated evolutionary rather than revolutionary change in Negro status, winning both praise and criticism from Negroes and whites.

20. White, William Allen. *The Autobiography of William Allen White*. Macmillan. 1946. 649 pp. $3.75.

As editor of the Emporia, Kansas *Gazette*, White became famous as the respected voice of small-town mid-western, middle class American society. Therefore, his autobiography reflects not only the work of a leading journalist but also the situation of a large part of American society between 1875 and 1925. White didn't live to complete his autobiography beyond the middle 1920's. Published posthumously, it won a Pulitzer prize in 1947.

21. Wright, Wilbur and Orville. *Miracle at Kitty Hawk: The Letters of Wilbur and Orville Wright*. Edited by Fred C. Kelly. Farrar, Straus and Young. 1951. 482 pp. (o. p.).

Over six hundred letters arranged chronologically to tell the story of the Wright brothers' contributions to the development of aviation. Air and space minded youngsters can learn much from the thoroughness of the Wright brothers' preparation and experimentation and the matter-of-fact way in which they recorded their accomplishments.

E. Individual Accounts Concerned Chiefly With Some Part of the Period 1920 to the Present.

1. Anderson, Mary. *Woman at Work: The Autobiography of Mary Anderson*. (As told to Mary Winslow). University of Minnesota. 1951.

Mary Anderson came to America from Sweden at the age of sixteen. She devoted her life to improving conditions for women workers and was director of the Women's Bureau of the United States Department of Labor from 1919 to 1944. Her story is most interesting and informative when she tells of her early years as a worker.

2. Byrnes, James F. *All In One Lifetime*. Harper. 1958. 473 pp. $5.00.

The life story of an influential southern politician. It is

most valuable when Byrnes discusses the conferences of foreign ministers he attended while serving as President Truman's Secretary of State, 1945–1947.

3. Calvert, James. *Surface at the Pole*. McGraw-Hill. 1960. 312 pp. $4.95.

Written by the commander of the *Skate*, this is the story of the way in which the nuclear submarine cruised under Arctic seas and then crashed through thin ice to emerge at the North Pole. Readers will get a good picture of polar geography from this book.

4. Connelly, W. L. *The Oil Business as I Saw It*. University of Oklahoma. 1954. 177 pp. $3.75.

Connelly held almost every kind of job in the American oil industry, working in all the great oil fields of Pennsylvania, Ohio, Texas, Oklahoma, Kansas, and in foreign lands over a period of sixty years. His brief but interesting recollections are for young men who like oil.

5. DeMille, Cecil B. *The Autobiography of Cecil B. DeMille*. Edited by Donald Hayne. Prentice-Hall. 1959. 514 pp. $5.95.

Describes the career of one of moving pictures' greatest producer-directors. This book has profuse information about the early days of moving pictures and the fantastic world of Hollywood during the 1920's and 1930's.

6. Dufek, Rear Admiral George F. *Operation Deepfreeze*. Harcourt, Brace. 1957. 334 pp. $5.00.

Admiral Dufek commanded Task Force 43 in Operation Deepfreeze, our Navy's expedition to Antarctica in support of the International Geophysical Year. His story of the expedition shows that exploration and adventure are still possible on this earth.

7. Eisenhower, Dwight D. *Crusade in Europe*. Doubleday. 1948. Cloth cover, $4.50. Garden City Perma Books. Paperback, 50¢.

The personal narrative of the Supreme Commander, Allied Expeditionary Forces. The narrative begins with the author's departure from the Philippines in 1940 and ends with the postwar occupation of Germany. It tells mainly of the high-level planning and co-ordination necessary for the

African, Italian, and Normandy invasions during World War II.

8. Farley, James A. *Behind the Ballots.* Harcourt, Brace. 1938. 392 pp. (o. p.).

A candid political memoir, this gives a realistic picture of a master of American political practices. It deals mainly with the aggressive campaign which Farley and Louis Howe conducted for eighteen months to secure Franklin D. Roosevelt's nomination at the 1932 Democratic convention. Also described are the methods used to win Roosevelt his landslide victory in the 1936 election.

9. Lindbergh, Charles A. *The Spirit of St. Louis.* Scribner. 1957. 562 pp. $5.95.

In 1927 Lindbergh became a popular hero when he flew across the Atlantic from New York to Paris. His autobiography, which centers around this episode, is a close-up view of American aviation during the first third of the twentieth century.

10. Morris, James. *As I Saw the U. S. A.* Pantheon. 1956. 384 pp. $3.95.

A modern-day travel account, written by a young English journalist who came to study the United States in the 1950's. Morris is especially good when assaying the influence of the automobile on American society.

11. Mauldin, William Henry (Bill). *Up Front.* Holt. 1945. 228 pp. (o. p.).

Bill Mauldin achieved fame as a war cartoonist in World War II and then as an author. This book is his story of the common soldier of World War II, based largely on the author's experiences in the European theater. It consists of both text and the most famous of his cartoons, which young people ought to get to know.

12. Perkins, Frances. *The Roosevelt I Knew.* Viking. 1946. 408 pp. (o. p.).

This book about the President was written by his Secretary of Labor, the first woman ever to serve in a Cabinet position. It contains her sympathetic, honest, and perceptive reminiscences and is particularly valuable because she knew

Roosevelt when he began his political career as a young man in the New York State Legislature.

13. Pyle, Ernie T. *Brave Men*. Holt. 1944. 399 pp. $3.00.

A collection of newspaper articles written about the common soldier in the European theater of World War II. Ernie Pyle was the most famous correspondent of that war and reached a large mass audience through his portrayal of the unsung heroes of conflict.

14. Robinson, Jackie. *My Own Story*. (As told to Wendell Smith.) Greenberg. 1948. 274 pp. (o. p.).

The story of the first Negro baseball player to break the color barrier in organized baseball. It is a good baseball story as well as a great drama of race relations.

15. Roosevelt, Eleanor. *Autobiography*. Harper. 1961. 623 pp. $6.95.

The complete story of the life of Mrs. Roosevelt. Her autobiography contains some of the material previously published in her books. These earlier books are: *On My Own: The Years Since the White House*. (Harper, 1958. $4.00); *This Is My Story* (Harper, 1937. $5.75); and *This I Remember* (Harper, 1949. $6.50). The last two are available in paperback. (Doubleday. 95¢.)

16. Truman, Harry S. *Memoirs*. Doubleday. 1955–56. Two Volumes. $6.50 each.

A very detailed personal report of Truman's years in the President's office. Volume I, *Year of Decision*, deals mainly with the momentous issues confronting Truman when World War II ended in 1945. Volume II, *Years of Trial and Hope*, vigorously defends the Truman administration's program for converting from war to peace while undergoing the financial drain of emergency relief to Europe and the Far East.

AUTHOR AND EDITOR INDEX

(Authors of Firsthand Literature Are Indicated by Capitalizing
Their Names)

DUFEK, GEORGE F., *Operation Deepfreeze*, 26

EGGLESTON, GEORGE CARY, *A Rebel's Recollections* (int., David Donald), 18

EISENHOWER, DWIGHT D., *Crusade in Europe*, 26–27

Eisenschiml, Otto, *American Iliad* (with Ralph Newman), 9; *Eyewitness* (with Ralph Newman), 9

Emrich, Duncan, *Comstock Bonanza*, 10

FARLEY, JAMES A., *Behind the Ballots*, 27

FORTEN, CHARLOTTE, *Journal of Charlotte F. Forten* (ed., Ray Allen Billington), 16

FRANKLIN, BENJAMIN, *Autobiography*, 14

FREMANTLE, JAMES ARTHUR LYON, *Fremantle Diary* (ed., Walter Lord), 18–19

GARLAND, HAMLIN, *Son of the Middle Border*, 22

GOMPERS, SAMUEL, *Seventy Years of Life and Labor* (eds., Philip Taft and J. A. Sessions), 22

Graham, W. A., *Custer Myth*, 10

Grant, William L., *Voyages of Samuel de Champlain, 1604–1618*, 6

GRANT, ULYSSES S., *Personal Memoirs* (ed., E. B. Long), 19

GREEN, JOHN, *Johnny Green of the Orphan Brigade* (ed., Albert D. Kirwan), 19

Hall, Clayton C., *Narratives of Early Maryland, 1633–1684*, 6

HALSTEAD, MURAT, *Three Against Lincoln* (ed. and int., William B. Hesseltine), 19–20

HAMILTON, DR. ALEXANDER, *Gentleman's Progress* (ed. and int., Carl Bridenbaugh), 14–15

Hamilton, Charles, *Cry of the Thunderbird*, 10

Handlin, Oscar, *This Was America*, 8

Hart, Albert B., *American History Told By Contemporaries*, 5

Harwell, Richard B., *Confederate Reader*, 9; *Union Reader*, 9

Hodge, Frederick W., *Spanish Explorers in the Southern United States, 1528–1543* (with T. H. Lewis), 6

HOOVER, HERBERT, *Memoirs of Herbert Hoover*, 22

Hosmer, James K., *Winthrop's Journal "History of New England," 1630–1649*, 6

HOUSTON, SAM, *Autobiography of Sam Houston* (eds., D. Day and H. H. Ullom), 16

James, Bartlett B., *Journal of Jasper Danckaerts, 1679–1680* (with J. F. Jameson), 6

Jameson, J. Franklin, *Edward Johnson's "Wonder-working Providence," 1628–1651*, 6; *Narratives of New Nederland, 1609–1664*, 6; *Original Narratives of Early American History*, 5–6

JEFFERSON, ISAAC, *Memoirs of a Monticello Slave* (ed., Rayford W. Logan), 16

JEFFERSON, THOMAS, *Autobiography* (int., Dumas Malone), 15

JONES, JOHN B., *Rebel War Clerk's Diary* (ed., Earl Schenck Miers), 20

Jones, Katherine M., *Heroines of Dixie*, 9

Kellogg, Louise P., *Early Narratives of the Northwest, 1634–1699*, 6

Kogan, Bernard R., *Chicago Haymarket Riot*, 13

LE CONTE, EMMA, *When the World Ended* (ed., Earl Schenck Miers), 20

LEWIS, MERIWETHER and WILLIAM CLARK, *Journals of Lewis and Clark* (ed., Bernard De Voto), 16–17

Lewis, Oscar, *Autobiography of the West*, 11

Lincoln, Charles H., *Narratives of the Indian Wars, 1675–1699*, 6

LINDBERGH, CHARLES A., *Spirit of St. Louis*, 27

McCormick, Edgar L., *Life on a Whaler* (with E. G. McGehee), 13

McDonnell, Robert F., *Modern America Through Foreign Eyes* (with W. E. Morris), 13

Z
1236
.B89
no.45

119264

MAN COLLEGE LIBRARY

PAMPHLETS *Published by the*

SERVICE CENTER FOR TEACHERS OF HISTORY

1. *Key to the Past: Some History Books for Pre-College Readers*, 3rd ed., by MARGARETA FAISSLER
2. *New Interpretations in American Foreign Policy*, 2nd ed., by ALEXANDER DeCONDE
3. *The South in American History*, 2nd ed., by OTIS A. SINGLETARY AND KENNETH K. BAILEY
4. *Industrial Revolution: Interpretations and Perspectives*, by ERIC E. LAMPARD
5. *Civil War and Reconstruction*, 2nd ed., by HAL BRIDGES
6. *The American Revolution: A Review of Changing Interpretations*, by EDMUND S. MORGAN
7. *The Colonial Period in Latin American History*, by CHARLES GIBSON
8. *The American Frontier*, 2nd ed., by RAY A. BILLINGTON
9. *Jacksonian Demoncracy*, by CHARLES G. SELLERS, JR.
10. *The Progressive Movement, 1900–1920: Recent Ideas and New Literature*, 2nd ed., by GEORGE E. MOWRY
11. *Greek and Roman History*, 2nd ed., by MORTIMER CHAMBERS
12. *The Middle West*, 2nd ed., by HARRY R. STEVENS
13. *History of Science*, 2nd ed., by MARIE BOAS HALL
14. *The Nature and Practice of State and Local History*, by PHILIP D. JORDAN
15. *Chinese History: A Bibliographic Review*, by CHARLES O. HUCKER
16. *New Interpretations of American Colonial History*, 2nd ed., by LOUIS B. WRIGHT
17. *The History of India: Its Study and Interpretation*, 2nd. ed., by ROBERT I. CRANE
18. *The Interpretation of Renaissance Humanism*, by WILLIAM J. BOUWSMA
19. *Recent Trends and New Literature in Canadian History*, by ROBIN W. WINKS
20. *Nationalism: Interpreters and Interpretations*, 2nd ed., by BOYD C. SHAFER
21. *The Background of the French Revolution*, by STANLEY J. IDZERDA
22. *A Style of History for Beginners*, by PAUL L. WARD
23. *The Middle Ages in Recent Historical Thought: Selected Topics*, 2nd ed., by BRYCE LYON
24. *The Near and Middle East: An Introduction To History and Bibliography*, by RODERIC H. DAVISON
25. *The New Deal in Historical Perspective*, 2nd ed., by FRANK FREIDEL
26. *The Far West in American History*, 2nd ed., by HARVEY L. CARTER
27. *Five Images of Germany: Half a Century of American Views on German History*, by HENRY CORD MEYER
28. *Great Britain in the Twentieth Century*, by HENRY R. WINKLER
29. *Nineteenth-Century Europe—Crisis and Contribution*, 2nd ed., by EUGENE N. ANDERSON
30. *American Intervention: 1917 and 1941*, by ERNEST R. MAY
31. *United States History: A Bridge to the World of Ideas* (A Syllabus), by W. BURLIE BROWN
32. *Normalcy and Reaction, 1921–1933: An Age of Disillusionment*, by JOHN D. HICKS
33. *The European Peasantry from the Fifteenth to the Nineteenth Century*, by JEROME BLUM
34. *Japanese History: New Dimensions of Approach and Understanding*, by JOHN WHITNEY HALL
35. *The Age of Reinterpretation*, by C. VANN WOODWARD
36. *The British Empire-Commonwealth: Its Themes and Character; a Plural Society in Evolution*, by CHARLES F. MULLETT
37. *Civil Rights: Retrospect and Prospects*, by CHASE C. MOONEY
38. *Some Elements of East European History*, by R. V. BURKS
39. *Military History*, by WALTER MILLIS
40. *The Federal Age, 1789–1829: America in the Process of Becoming*, by KEITH B. BERWICK
41. *Marxism Since the Communist Manifesto*, by ALFRED G. MEYER
42. *Latin American History Since 1825*, 2nd ed., by ARTHUR P. WHITAKER

(Continued on cover 3)

Withdrawn by
Whitman College Library

HEY WERE THERE

A GUIDE TO FIRSTHAND LITERATURE FOR USE IN TEACHING AMERICAN HISTORY

by RICHARD C. BROWN
State University of New York College at Buffalo

Publication Number 45

SERVICE CENTER FOR TEACHERS OF HISTORY

A Service of the American Historical Association
400 A Street, S. E. Washington, D. C. 20003

36
39
45

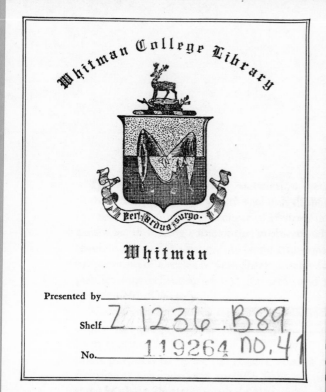

Whitman College Library

Whitman

Presented by_____

Shelf Z 1236 .B89

No. 119264 no.41

...ause of its continuing interest ...United States, has established ...an effort to offer constructive ...ich today beset the classroom ...d by the Service Center is the ...taining a concise summary of ...new interpretations in a par-

...e neither the time nor oppor- ...ature, these pamphlets have ...teachers' needs. Each pam- ...f current interpretations and ...torical study. Our aim is, in ...y keeping up to date in their fields of interest. It is our sincere hope that this will materially benefit the teacher and thereby contribute to the enrichment of classroom instruction. The extent to which the project is successful will be measured by the degree to which the regrettable gap between the teacher of history in the school and the specialist in historical research is narrowed.

WALTER RUNDELL, JR.
Assistant Executive Secretary
American Historical Association